SCOTTISH

Sweetie Addicts

and

CHOCOHOLICS

Deedee Cuddihy

First Published 2019
Copyright©2019 by Deedee Cuddihy

ISBN 978 0 9930986 5 9

Published by Deedee Cuddihy
10 Otago Street,
Glasgow G12 8JH
Scotland

Cover design and technical
assistance: The Lodger (Glasgow)
Ltd.

Printed in Glasgow by Bell and Bain Ltd

Dedication

This book is dedicated to the many people who so generously shared their sweeties and chocolate stories with me. In particular I would like to thank the (late) Giffnock Friendship Club, Caryl Godwin (again!); Iain Scott and family; members of Merchant Voices choir; my "Shapenotes" chums; Hillhead Library book group and, last but not least, Iain at GOMA in Glasgow for his terrrific tale of having his tooth pulled out *after* the dentist had smoked a fag!

Foreword

Having been brought up in America, I was not at all familiar with the traditional, Scottish-style sweetie shops when I moved here as a teenager back in the early 1960s. Jars of things called "boilings" and "gums" which were weighed on scales and slipped into little paper bags, may well have existed in my native New York when my parents were young. But by the time I was buying "candy" (as we called it), it was all branded and ready-wrapped. I never did develop a liking for delicacies such as Soor Plooms, Lucky Tatties, Dolly Mixture and Midget Gems. But I did become very fond of Marathon Bars (and will not call them Snickers!), Bounty Bars and Opal Fruits (*not* Starburst!). And Chocolate Oranges. And, more recently, tablet. And I did become "hooked" on nuts and raisins which could also be bought in sweetie shops for, I think, 6d a quarter. Oddly enough, and despite having been resident in Scotland for more than five decades, I didn't realise until I started research for this book that the term "sweeties" didn't encompass chocolate. Every day is, indeed, a school day!

I'm Scottish - of course I like sweeties! On a Friday, my dad used to come in from work with a bag of sweets for me and my brother - all the usual ones that were around in the 1960s. But I prefer chocolate these days - it's easier on the fillings than toffee. I especially like the really good Italian brands. My husband also likes chocolate. He's got Parkinson's and says it helps lift his mood.

(Ruth)

I was a voracious eater of sweets when I was a child, especially of chocolate. Cadbury's milk chocolate was my favourite - not with fruit and nuts; that would have been a waste of the space where chocolate could have been, as far as I was concerned. We got Quality Street at Christmas. I liked the purple ones best, followed by the caramels and then the orange ones. All the rest were a bit rubbish. Then there were those bracelets with the sweeties on them that you could eat off your wrist. And Lucky Bags - with Dolly Mixture and a toy!

(Fiona)

I've always loved chocolate. My mum was a good cook and until I left home 30 years ago, I had a really well-balanced diet. Now I'd say it's about 70 per cent chocolate-based! Already today I've eaten a Thorntons chocolate bar and I've just opened a bag of their champagne truffles. I'll have to change my ways or I'll end up with diabetes!

(woman in a cafe, eating chocolate)

I like all sweeties but particularly marshmallows. I can easily eat a whole packet in one go and start on another. They've always been my favourite, especially the pink ones. I don't deliberately choose to eat the pink ones first but I do feel a "yes!" moment when I pull a pink one from the bag instead of a white one.

(Hannah)

I've always preferred chocolate to sweeties, even when I was a young girl. Although I used to buy a 10 pence mix from the ice cream van when it came 'round - things like cola cubes and cola bottles. And one of my favourite presents ever was a miniature sweetie shop that my uncle got me one year for my birthday. It had wee bottles of sweets and scales that your could weigh them on.

(woman in a library, eating chocolate)

I used to buy "Lucky Potatoes" -
those big, round soft sweeties with
cinnamon on the outside and a wee
toy inside. They couldn't do that
nowadays. They'd be too worried
that a kid would choke on it.

*I thought they were called "Lucky
Tatties"?*

Well, we called them "Lucky
Potatoes" in Lenzie, where I came
from.

(Liz)

I've got two brothers and a sister and we ate masses of sweets when I was growing up on Arran, especially chocolate bars because we had a shop and my dad would bring home the chocolate that was coming up to its "use by" date, particularly Bounty bars which he liked but I didn't. My favourite was Dairy Milk. I can remember reading in bed at night and eating chocolate - after I'd brushed my teeth! None of us ever got fat because we were always running around outside. But I've got diabetes now - and no wonder!

(Judy)

I've got five brothers and sisters so any sweets that were brought into the house when I was growing up didn't last long. I remember a girl moved in across the road from us who only had one sibling. She invited me over for my tea one day and I was amazed to discover that they had a big jar of sweets in the kitchen that she and her brother could just dip into whenever they wanted. I'd never seen anything like it!

(Louisa)

I can go months with no chocolates but then I get a notion and go hard on them for a few days!

(Ruby)

I sometimes do a Pick 'n' Mix for the bath. I've got a little metal bowl that floats and I put some Haribo and chocolate buttons in it - and maybe some of those strawberry sweets. It's just 10 minutes of "me" time away from the kids.

(Rosie)

My wife really likes chocolate but it gives her migraines and she has to go lie down. I say to her: *"If you eat that chocolate you'll have a headache tonight!"* but she does it anyway.

(Bill)

I prefer sweeties to chocolate: treacle toffee, cream caramels, Polly Pastilles . . . And as a child, I ate gums, midget gems and jelly babies. You'd only get chocolate on special occasions in those days, like a Fry's chocolate bar in your stocking at Christmas - the one with five different flavours.

(Jen)

I'm a chocoholic and so is my husband. We hoped our son wouldn't be one but no such luck - he loves it too! I really like milk chocolate so I've switched to dark chocolate to help me cut down. Now I just have milk chocolate as an occasional "treat".

(woman in Thorntons buying £28 worth of chocolate)

I have a deep appreciation of anything with sugar on it which was one of the main reasons why I started going out with a guy who was a friend of one of my pals. She was meeting him for a drink and asked me to come too and as he walked up to us, he held out a paper bag and said: "Anyone want a Jelly Snake?" I did, of course . . . Even better - it turned out that he owned two sweetie shops! I never got fed up watching him make big pans of tablet to put on sale but the relationship eventually fizzled out.

(Helen)

My first job when I left school, age 15, was at Buchanan's sweetie factory in Glasgow, getting £2, 10 shillings a week. I was the office junior and I had to run all over the city, taking bills of lading to shipping offices like the Anchor Line in St. Vincent Place, because they sent sweeties all over the world. We weren't allowed to eat the sweets - that was a sackable offence and meant instant dismissal. But when I went down to the factory floor, the women who worked there would slip me a few wee sweeties and I had to eat them on the stairs before I went back up to the office so I wouldn't get caught.

(Ann)

I used to help my husband run a sweetie shop he bought in the Gorbals, in Eglinton Street, not long after he came back from the war. It was so long ago, I can't remember the name of it! But it was situated between two cinemas - the Coliseum and the Bedford - so business was very good for the first few years, with people queueing up to buy sweets before going to the pictures.

Sweets were still on ration then so you sold what you were given by the suppliers. Our local wholesaler was Italian and John had been stationed in Italy and could speak the language so that helped.

Then we got lucky when John met a chocolate maker who supplied shops like Harrods but had decided to retire and was selling his stock. That included great big slabs of very high quality chocolate couverture which because it was a covering and not an actual sweet, could be sold "off ration".

We laid it out on wallpaper pasting tables in our spare room, broke it into pieces with a toffee hammer, weighed it into quarters and put it into bags to sell in the shop and it went like a bomb!

(Chris)

In the late 1960s, you could work when you were 14 and I had two after-school jobs, one in a cafe and one in a sweetie shop on Paisley Road West which also sold newspapers and tobacco. I was terrible for sweeties and you could eat as many as you wanted. That was one of the perks of the job and wasn't considered stealing. I was the eldest of nine children and when my brothers and sisters came in, I'd maybe slip them two penny dainties instead of the one they were paying for - as long as Bessie and Bunty, the two old ladies who ran the shop, weren't looking.

(Maureen)

When you get old, you start wanting the sweets you used to eat when you were children. We've just bought almost £20 worth including some Hawick Balls - because I'm from Hawick!

(Married couple in Mitchell's sweet shop, Glasgow)

I had a Saturday job from the age of 14 until I went away to university, at R. Walker Brown's tobacconist and sweet shop in Galashiels. That was a dream job for me because I loved sweeties - and so did my dad. I started at £1.75 a day for a three week trial and then it went up to £3, working 9-5.30 one Saturday and 9-6 the next. My pal already worked there and our first job in the morning was to dust the sweetie jars when Mr. Brown went up to get his breakfast.

That's when we used to eat the sweeties! We had to wipe the jars down with a damp cloth, getting on step ladders to reach the high shelves that went all the way up to the ceiling.

When they got some new sweeties in, Mr. Brown's wife would say to us:"Have you tried one of these yet?" and we'd say: "Oh, no . . . " even though we had - and she knew it!

(Anne)

Far too many sugary things are eaten these days. It's not good for you so when my grandchildren come over for a visit and want to know if I've got any sweeties, I say: *"I don't keep poison in the house!"*

(Rosella)

My mother was quite strict about what we ate and most of our requests for sweets were met with the offer of a raw carrot. Or, on rare occasions, a stick of rhubarb that we were allowed to dip in sugar.

(Ann C.)

Ally, bally, ally bally bee,
Sittin' on yer mammy's knee
Greetin' for a wee bawbee,
Tae buy some Coulter's candy.

We had no sweets in our house when I was young. In primary school, at break time, my play piece was an apple! I used to look enviously at all the other children eating sweets and crisps. Having an apple meant you couldn't take part in one-for-one "swopsies", where you'd swop one crisp for a sweet. I mean, you couldn't do that with an apple!

But when I started secondary school, I'd stop off at the Buck's Head Cafe in Clarkston almost every day on my way home and buy a packet of Cadbury's Dark Silk - five individual strawberry cream chocolates that were just delicious. I don't know why they stopped making them!

(Rhona)

My daughter has joked that, if Thorntons ever stop making her favourite Viennese truffles, she's going to set herself on fire outside one of their shops in protest.

(Gillian)

My father used to make us coconut ice, toffee and tablet. It was just something he did. I think his own father used to make sweets as well. The tablet was delicious.

(Robert)

My father was a welder
and he'd suddenly take it
into his head to make
toffee balls or tablet. It
was just something he
liked to do from time to
time.

(Joe)

My dad who was a brick layer in a big construction company, had a real sweet tooth and when he got in from work, Monday to Thursday, he'd give each of the five of us one sweetie, usually a cube of toffee wrapped in a bit of paper, and then on a Friday - pay day - we'd get a bar of chocolate each.

(Kathleen)

I was brought up by my grandparents and whenever I come back home to Stirling from uni for the weekend, my gran always has the desk in my room laid out with sweeties and chocolate, as well as crisps and wee bottles of Irn-Bru. When I was growing up, buying sweets was something all the kids in the area did on a daily basis, usually spending about a pound. And when a Lidl opened near the school, we could buy even more because the sweets they sold were so cheap, including a bar of chocolate for just 18 pence.

(Michael)

I grew up in Glasgow and there was a woman near us who sold toffee apples from a window in her house.

(Karen)

Near where I lived, there was a woman on the ground floor in an old tenement who made sweeties and sold them from her house: candy cakes and toffee and black stripe balls . . . And when school came out, you'd go 'round and chap on her back window if you wanted to buy something.

(Jean)

I'm from Blackwood in Lanarkshire and I can remember there used to be people in the village who made tablet and toffee apples in their homes and if you wanted any, you went to their door and bought it.

(Frank)

A boy at our primary school used to buy big bags of sweets for his lunch every day - Fried Eggs and that kind of thing. He never ate sandwiches, and he *was* fat. But he was very generous with his sweets if you asked him for one.

(Sarah)

There was a craze at our primary school to see how many Atomic Fire Balls you could cram into your mouth at one time. They were incredibly spicy and everyone in the playground would be going around with red drool dripping down their chins. I think the record was 45.

(Carla)

The big difference between the pupils at the high school I went to and the ones at the nearby private school was that, in the local sweet shop at lunch time, we'd be buying the cheap stuff from plastic boxes on the counter - doing rapid calculations with the small change in our pockets to see what we could afford - and they'd be buying branded chocolate bars, and paying with pound notes and even fivers.

(Robin)

Where chewing in class was concerned, I remember at primary school our teacher would say: *"Are you eating a sweet, Gary?"* - because it was usually Gary Thomson - and then she would ask: *"Do you have enough for everyone?"* Of course the answer was always "no" so then she would tell him: *"Well - stop eating!"*

(Iona)

The first and only time I ever got the belt was for eating sweeties, when I was 14. I usually had a bag of Midget Gems in my pocket - the liquorice ones were my favourites - and I must have put one in my mouth without thinking about it and the next thing, the teacher called me out and gave me one of the belt. Around 15 years later, I was enrolling my son at primary school and the headmaster turned out to be the same teacher! He said he remembered me but didn't remember giving me the belt.

(Muriel)

We got sweets everyday on our way back from school. Everyone could afford to buy something because there was not only a penny tray at the shop we went to but a half-penny tray as well.

(Angela)

I can remember there was a sweet shop right opposite New Stevenston primary school (in Lanarkshire). It was a kind of wooden hut with a rounded roof and no floor, set on some tarmac at the bottom of someone's garden.

I think a woman ran it but it was difficult to tell because she wore a sort of helmet. It was open at lunch time and after school and all the kids went.

It wasn't jars of sweets but boxes, laid out on the counter, with penny caramels and Highland Toffee and various types of liquorice.

I got thrupence a week for sweets which bought a lot: four caramels for a penny, for instance. Some children only got a penny and a very few got sixpence which was riches!

(Charlie)

There was a woman in Larkhall who had a long garden at the back of her house with a hut at the bottom of it and she ran it as a sweetie shop. That's because it was right beside the road out of Larkhall Academy and all the pupils had to walk past it on their way to and from the school. She didn't sell anything fancy - mostly boilings and gums.

(Norma)

I remember the time I was queueing up to pay for a Fizzy Bomb jaw breaker-type sweet at Jessie and Jack's shop on Victoria Road and I had already started crunching on it when I felt one of my teeth at the back crack and the worst pain I'd ever experienced shot through me.

I ran out of the shop and straight along to the dentist's at Queen's Park where I'd been only a few weeks before. The receptionist said: *"Have you been eating sweeties again?"*

The dentist saw me right away and smoked a fag while she waited for the anesthetic to kick in before she pulled my tooth out.

To make matters worse, there was a chap on our door that night and it was Jessie from the shop, telling my mum I hadn't paid for the Fizzy Bomb. So I got a slap on the back of my legs for that!

(Iain)

I was addicted to sweeties when I was wee. It didn't matter what kind of sweeties - I'd gobble them up. But I didn't like chocolate. When I got an Easter egg, I'd eat the sweeties from it and give the egg to my sister. But when I had kids, I tried not to eat so many sweeties because I didn't want them ending up like me - with no teeth!

(John)

I remember going to our local paper shop in Glasgow and getting those boiled sweet lollipops in corrugated tinfoil which did my milk teeth in, resulting in me having to visit the dentist to get those blackened stumps pulled out - absolute agony!

(Rob, from an email)

My curse upon your venom'd stang,
That shoots my tortur'd gums alang,
An' thro' my lug gies mony a twang,
Wi' gnawing vengeance,
Tearing my nerves wi' bitter pang,
Like racking engines!

("Address To The Toothache" by Robert Burns)

"Can I get a lollipop, mummy?"
"No!"
"Can I please get a lollipop,
mummy?"
"No - you don't get a lollipop
for going to the dentist!"

(mum to her young son leaving the
dentist)

A whole generation of parents has grown up thinking dried fruit such as raisins are always a healthier alternative to sweets and chocolate – but it's not true. Dentists loathe dried fruit because it's full of sugar and so sticky that it sits on the teeth, effectively burning through the enamel and rotting them. While they wouldn't claim that chocolate was healthy, it is dentally safer. "The best treat is something that washes away quickly – that's why chocolate is better than dried fruit," said a dental expert.

(from a news report)

We were very sweetie deprived in our family and chewing gum, in particular, was not allowed, so much so that if we found a piece of gum stuck to the pavement outside our house, we'd pick it up, wash it under the tap and chew it ourselves! We were especially pleased if it was pink because that meant bubble gum which was a real treat. But I was only six or seven at the time.

(Eilidh)

I'm from China and we don't have shops where you can buy sweets and chocolate like you do here. You can get imported Cadbury's but that's £5 a bar and a Toblerone is £15! When I went home on a visit last year, I spent almost £200 on chocolate - Cadbury's and Thorntons and Toblerone and Ferrero Rocher - as presents for all my family and friends. My father still has some of the chocolate I brought him. He keeps it in the fridge and has one piece a day, because it's good for his health.

(Winnie)

I have a lovely German friend who, every Christmas, sends us gifts of chocolate-covered marzipan, the problem being that, as a family, we're not that keen on marzipan which once resulted in a large, chocolate-covered marzipan Santa bought for my son eventually ending up on the compost heap!

(Rosa)

In Ukraine, where I'm from, most cities have a factory where chocolate and sweets are made. When he was at university, my father - who has the real sweet tooth in our family - worked at the local chocolate factory during the holidays.

The rule then was you couldn't take anything out of the factory but you could eat as much as you wanted inside.

Later on, during the Soviet era,
people who worked in the
factories would sneak out blocks
of cocoa mass to sell locally,
because it was delicious and
very sought after.

They also smuggled out cocoa
butter which you'd mix into
warm milk for a lovely, soothing
drink when you had a cough or a
cold.

(Natalia)

In Azerbaijan, where I come from, we had what we called Moscow chocolate, because it was from Russia. It was chocolate with nuts and raisins in it and my grandmother, in particular, liked it very much. And we had chocolate from Ukraine which is also famous for being very good. Now my husband has found the same kind of nuts and raisins chocolate here in Glasgow that we had in Azerbaijan - and we're eating it all the time!

(Aya)

"Everyone's a Fruit and Nut case . . . "

(1970s advertising jingle)

My son used to sell sweets 'round the doors when he was a teenager, for pocket money. It was macaroon bars and tablet etc. I'm not sure where he got it. I think someone in a van came around and organised it.

(Sheila)

You used to get people coming 'round the doors with tablet and coconut ice and macaroon bars and one day this boy I really fancied from school shows up at our door selling sweeties. I was in S1 and he was three or four years older and wouldn't even have noticed me and I was like *"Yes, mum - buy some and get him to come back next week as well!"*

(Susan)

When I was in high school, I remember making macaroon bars in Home Economics using mashed potato which is traditional but you'd never have known from the taste that it was one of the ingredients.

(Pat)

In 2015, at Shetland's annual food fair, Dave Williams used local algae to create Seaweed Chocolate which was an instant hit and led to the formation of *"Mirrie Dancers"*, one of the UK's most northerly chocolatiers.

(from the internet)

Graham Donaldson, owner of Crieff-based sweetie business, Gordon & Durward, recalls as a boy visiting a local farm, and being told as he was handed a sweetie from the farmer's fluffy pocket to *"spit the first sook oot."* Despite this, a sweet tooth and a love of Scottish sweeties developed.

(from the internet)

The most troubling addiction within Bros was the five-a-day Boost bar habit of Craig *"Ken"* Logan who came from Kirkcaldy.

(from Sylvia Patterson's book *"I'm not with the Band".)*

My brother, Jonathan is addicted to Crunchies. He was home for a holiday recently and spent all his time in the sitting room, watching repeats of "Top Gear". After he left, we discovered a foot-deep layer of Crunchie bar wrappers behind the sofa.

(Annie)

I suppose I had quite sophisticated tastes for a child - preferring dark chocolate to milk - and from about the age of 10, I got a box of either Terry's "All Gold" or "Black Magic" every Christmas, all to myself, wrapped up under the tree.

(Alison)

Eastern European Pic 'n' Mix in
Glasgow shop

Allan Tall's pic of his mum,
Elizabeth, at Barbour's newsagent,
Byres Rd., circa 1965

Emergency on the Quality
Street counter

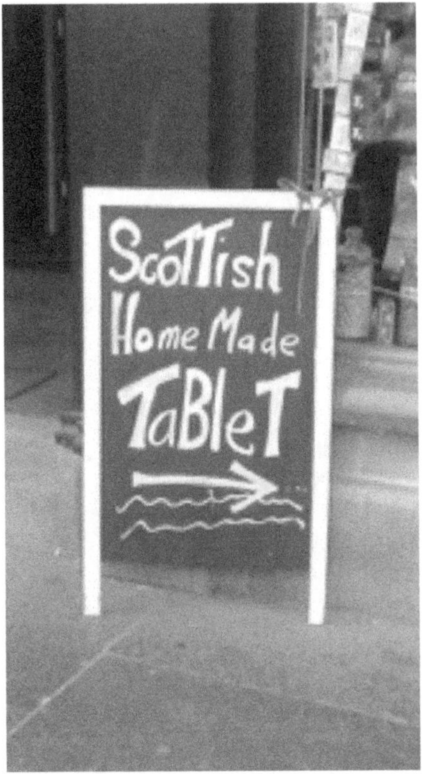
Scottish
Home Made
TabLeT

Birthday cake on St. Kilda

Dropped - unopened - Finger of Fudge

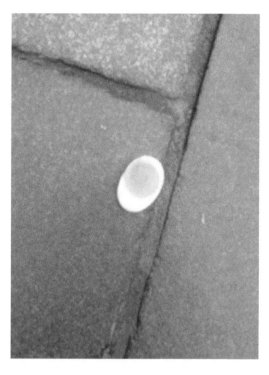

Dropped fried egg sweetie

Asian sweets shop

You used to be able to get Cadbury's Lucky Numbers from the sweets counter at Woolworth's, sold loose. They were like Roses or Quality Street but with numbers printed on the wrappers. And I'd always ask the girl who was serving me to try and put a lot of my favourite numbers in the bag.

(Nan)

*I can remember
when Walnut Whips
used to have a
walnut inside the
chocolate as well as
on the top of it.*

(Maggie)

We're all chocoholics here. We've got a special drawer that you can rummage in for a Galaxy or something when you're feeling peckish. I've got a friend who works in Vision Express and she says it's the same there. There must be something about opticians and chocolate . . .

(McGrath's, Byres Road, Glasgow)

There are always sweeties and chocolates on the go at the libraries I've worked in. As well as bringing them in ourselves, library users give us presents of chocolates at Christmas and as a "thank you" for something we've helped them with - although someone brought us in some fruit once which was unusual. At one branch, there was a tradition of bringing back sweets from wherever we'd been on holiday.

(Laura)

The life-expectancy of chocolates in UK hospitals is a short one - at least according to the results of a new study which found that when a box of chocolates was placed on a ward near sweet-toothed medical workers, it took them just 12 minutes before diving in and starting to eat. The rate of consumption only slowed down when all the popular chocolates had been taken.

(from a news report)

Sweets and chocolates were an essential part of nursing in my day, especially on the labour wards when you were doing long shifts and couldn't stop to eat.

You'd always have some sweets in your pocket to keep you going - and the mums! Haribo, wine gums, sherbet lemons, pan drops . . .

And a box of chocolates was a traditional gift that families would give to nursing staff as a "thank you". Thorntons were a particular treat.

The word would go around that a box of chocolates was on the go and the doctors would come in looking for one. You had to get there quickly or they'd all be eaten.

I remember in the neonatal unit in Dumfries we had a very ill baby who was there for a year and his mum brought him back for a visit every Christmas - until he was a teenager - with a tin of Roses chocolates for the staff.

(Meg, retired mid-wife)

Haribo Tangfastics got me through my first labour - all seven hours of it. My husband had to feed them to me because I was so off my face with morphine. But it turned out that he was eating even more of them than I was: basically one for me and two for him.

(Rosie)

There were three different names for what was basically a round, hard peppermint sweetie: they were generally known as Pan Drops; people with social pretentions called them Mint Imperials and in the village I came from outside Dundee, they were referred to as *Granny Sookers*.

That's because grannies *"sooked"* them in church so they wouldn't fall asleep during the sermon.

If you went through two *grannie sookers*, that was a measure of how dull a sermon had been. You didn't crunch them, of course, because you weren't supposed to eat anything in church.

As a child, I'd *sook* a mint with my head bent down, as if I was being terribly pious, but it was to prevent anyone seeing that I was eating a sweetie.

(Caryl)

One of the elders in our church always gets a sweetie out just before the sermon. I know that because you can always hear the sweetie paper crackling.

(Joy)

My gran was known in the family as *"Her Imperial Majesty"* because she always had some mint imperials in her pocket. I was a real fidget in church and she'd put her arm around me really tight - crushing me to her side - and stick a mint imperial in my mouth. I'd snuggle into her and just fall asleep, with the sweetie in my mouth, although they're supposed to keep you awake.

(Joan)

My mother-in-law had a story about going to a concert at the St. Andrew's Halls in Glasgow when a woman behind her started having a coughing fit. She turned around and discreetly passed her what she thought was a Mint Imperial that she had found in her coat pocket. She heard the woman spluttering a bit and at the interval she said to my mother-in-law: *"That was a moth ball you gave me - not a mint!"* Fortunately, she'd managed to spit it out before it did any damage.

(Denise)

Tablet (*taiblet* in Scots) is a medium-hard, sugary confection from Scotland. Tablet is usually made from sugar, condensed milk, and butter, which is boiled to a soft-ball stage and allowed to crystallise.

(wikipedia)

I buy a 2.5 kilo jar of Scottish Tablet every December as a Christmas gift for myself lol. The best before date is usually the middle of July the following year, which gives me about 7 or 8 months to finish it and I can guarantee that the jar is empty well before then!

(from the internet)

And a listener has contacted us to say that the most inappropiate Christmas present he ever received was a packet of whisky-infused tablet from his parents who, despite knowing he was a recovering alcoholic who had been sober for 10 years, couldn't understand what the problem was.

("Off the Ball" on BBC Radio Scotland)

One of our neighbours made tablet but we knew it as Swiss Milk Toffee which is what everyone in our area of Aberdeen called it.

(Jean)

I'm currently eating my way through a big box of Milk Tray that was a gift from my husband's cousin whose wife has just had twin boys. Traditionally, in Asian culture, couples give boxes of Indian sweets - *barfi* - to relatives and close friends to celebrate the birth of a baby - especially if it's a boy! But that's changing now and many parents are giving boxes of chocolates instead.

(Palo)

I run an Asian sweets shop in Glasgow and, these days, parents are buying barfi gift boxes for family and friends whether they've had a boy or a girl. We also sell barfi gift sets with a pink or a blue teddy to give to the new parents and we sell more of the pink ones than the blue ones.

(manager, barfi shop)

"The best way to describe *barfi* is like tablet, but not so sweet."

(Scottish food blogger, Pamela Timms, now based in Delhi)

Who knew you could make chocolate Fudge in a slow cooker !

(Karen, from Paisley, posting on Facebook)

I come from outside the UK and prefer salty snacks but my partner is Scottish and they really like chocolate, especially the high-quality brand I buy them from a specialist shop in Glasgow.

(young man talking about his non-binary partner's fondness for chocolate)

Dear Deedee,

Thank you for your email. The truth is I've never been a big one for sweets - but anything with salt and I am all over it. I do enjoy those squashie sweeties just now though...

Hope that helps in some way!

All the best,

Mhairi Black MP
Member of Parliament
Paisley and Renfrewshire South

I was brought up on the Isle of Lewis and, in those days, sweeties weren't available the way they were on the mainland. I remember the first sweetie I had, thinking it was disgusting. I could feel it doing something awful to my mouth.

(Rab)

My son has never had a sweet tooth, a fact that my sweetie-eating, late mother-in-law had great difficulty coming to terms with. She always brought him a tube of Fruit Gums when she came to visit and eventually, exasperated by his continuing lack of interest in them, she told me: *"I'm not buying David sweeties anymore because he doesn't seem to appreciate them!"*

(Margaret)

Scottish women who have found themselves on the wrong side of the law are turning their lives around by making luxury handmade chocolates. A pioneering new project based in a church near Stirling aims to boost their self-esteem and confidence and support them to find work. Joyce Murray, founder of community interest company Positive Changes which makes *Grace Chocolates*, said 20 women have engaged with the seven-week programme.

(from a news report)

My daughter can get very stressed when she's driving on a busy road and one afternoon recently I had to feed her Jelly Babies to calm her down while she negotiated the Edinburgh City Bypass. She needed the sugar to steady her nerves.

(Clair)

A driver from Peterhead has been banned from the road and fined £450 after eating a box of chocolate liqueurs containing high levels of vodka. The 27-year-old man was pulled over by police on his way home from a party in Fraserburgh. Despite protesting that he hadn't had a drink, a breathalyser reading showed he was nearly two and a half times over the legal alcohol limit.

(from a news report)

"Prisoners riot over shortage of Mars bars at Scotland's newest jail."

(news headline)

Yeah I stole sweeties all
the time. I'd send ma
mate to the magazine
rack then start filling
ma pockets while the
man was shouting at ma
pal for reading
magazines.

(Fraser, on Facebook)

This was in the late 1960s, when I was in P5 or 6, and at lunch time we'd go to Mrs. Manson's Dairy on Gt. Western Road where she sold her own home-made tablet which was very, very good but - at six pence a bar - quite expensive for children with limited pocket money.

So a pal of mine came up with the ingenious idea of painting a stash of old farthing coins silver and passing them off as sixpences. Farthings had been taken out of circulation several years earlier but they were roughly the same size as a sixpence and had been worth only a quarter of a penny.

I don't know how many bars of tablet he managed to buy with his counterfeit sixpences but one day Mrs. Manson came marching up to the school and although she couldn't identify the boy, she knew roughly how old he was.

The headmaster called an assembly and invited the culprit to step forward. Not surprisingly, he didn't but it caused quite a scandal and that was the end of my pal's forging career. At least, I assume it was . . .

(Iain S.)

A kind-hearted teenager has raised funds to ensure children living in poverty in Glasgow receive a festive treat for Christmas. The 15-year-old, from Paisley, gathered enough donations to buy 100 selection boxes which he donated to a food bank. *"Everyone deserves a selection box at Christmas"* he said.

(from a news story)

All my kids got a
Chocolate Orange at
Christmas - and they
still expect one,
even though they're
grown ups!

(June)

When I first started
working as a lollipop
man about eight years
ago, you used to get
boxes of chocolates - and
aftershave! - from the
kids at Christmas. But
that doesn't happen so
much now.

(Alan)

We were travellers from the Newcastle area and me mam used to spoil the five of us with chocolate at Christmas. She'd buy those special tins of Roses and Quality Street that you get at that time of year and put them in the window of our caravan instead of Christmas decorations because the colours were so bright. Then on Christmas morning, we'd sit on the bed and she'd get the first tin down and open it and we'd all dive in. She got us chocolate eggs at Easter, too.

(Billy the street preacher)

If there were no proper sweets available because of rationning, you could usually get cinnamon sticks - and liquorice root - from the chemist's or the sweetie shop. With cinnamon sticks, you'd pretend it was a cigarette but that didn't lead you onto smoking real cigarettes. They said the same thing about sweetie cigarettes but that was nonsense as well because I've never smoked.

(Jim)

We didn't get a lot of sweets - me and my brother and sister. But when Selection Boxes started being a thing at Christmas, and we were getting them from the grannies and the aunties, my mother took full control and doled the contents out to us in such a miserly way that they lasted until March! She'd take a Mars bar, for instance, and cut it into three bits and give us a piece each in our packed lunches for school but you couldn't eat it openly because that was just the sort of thing that could get you beaten up in the playground.

(John)

When I was a child, rationing was on and you'd use your sweetie ration for a Mars bar but you wouldn't eat the whole thing yourself. You'd take it home and slice it up so that everyone could have a piece of it.

(Isabel)

A Scottish taxi driver who put a 23-year-old Mars Bar up for sale on Facebook "for a laugh" was stunned when hundreds of people wanted to buy it. The man, from Peterhead, found the chocolate bar in his loft, with its 26p price sticker still attached. Within hours of posting it on-line, it had been snapped up for a fiver by a collector from Kirkcaldy who sent a courier to collect it.

(from a news story)

A Mars a day helps you work, rest and play.

(advertising slogan)

If you were only getting thrupence a week to spend on sweets, you wanted to get something that presented real value for money - and that was usually a Highland Toffee bar. It already had squares marked on it so you'd bash it on a kerbstone in the street to break it into bits and then suck each piece for as long as possible.

(Joyce)

"So there I was lying in the gutter. A man stopped and asked *"What's the matter? Did you fall over?"* So I said "No. I've a bar of toffee in my back pocket and I was just trying to break it." "

(the late Chic Murray, Scottish comedian, with thanks to Allan Tall)

They should be so lucky! Aussie singing sensation, Kylie Minogue leaves staff in an Aberdeenshire sweet shop 'spinning around' with a surprise visit to buy dolly mixtures and soor plooms.

(from the MailOnline, 2016)

When I was at boarding school in Edinburgh in 1956, we got a treat once a week on a Saturday of *one* sweet. And we were allowed to choose it ourselves! I always picked a Soor Ploom. I still drool every time I think of them and always try to buy some when I'm back in Scotland from Australia. P.S. Sweeties are called lollies here in Australia.

(Alec, from an email)

I'm trying to watch my weight but I've got a terrible weakness for those large bars of Bournville dark chocolate. When I start eating one, I can't stop until it's finished.

(John B.)

A *Curly Wurly* is great if you're slimming because it takes so much effort to eat one that you're almost into negative calories by the time you've finished.

(Caroline)

My sister can have a box of chocolates lying open in her house for a week or more and not eat them all. I couldn't do that! I'd have to eat them up asap.

(Kate)

Scottish women are the slimmest in the UK, despite the fact that they eat more chocolate than women south of the border, according to a health survey.

(from the internet)

During the Clydebank blitz, a bomb was dropped on a sweetie factory in the Oatlands area of Glasgow where I lived and the next day, we were all out there, scrabbling around in the rubble, looking for sweeties.

(Marlene)

"This was back in the 1950s but does anyone recall the fire that destroyed the sweetie warehouse between Lochend Road and Easter Road in Leith? I was at Leith Academy and it would have been about 8.30am when we descended like a pack of wild animals to get in past the firemen who, taking into account that the sweet ration was still very active, stepped aside to allow us free access to the remains. We spent the rest of the morning sitting in class, scraping the burned and singed bits off our booty to allow it to be eaten. Ah, happy days!

(Archie, posting on an internet forum)

We're very well provided with sweets at our Convent. When a family member comes to visit, they often bring a present of a box of chocolates and the Sister who receives it usually shares them with the rest of us. You wouldn't normally take a box of chocolates to your room and keep it to yourself.

(Sister Doreen)

Scots are terrible for eating chocolate: chocolate, chocolate, chocolate, all the time . . . We don't eat so many sweets in Texas where I come from. But my mom was from Glasgow and my gran used to send me a selection box every Christmas. I just didn't realise the extent of chocolate eating until I moved here.

(Gerry, from Texas)

Have you not heard of the well-known Scottish street preacher and evangelist, Jock Troup? He was famous for having such a loud voice that you could hear him from the top of Buchanan Street down to St. Enoch's. And he was also famous for being so addicted to chocolate that he told people: *"I prayed for deliverence from it . . . and God answered my prayers."* However, when he was later seen eating a piece of chocolate, he said: *"Surely God will forgive me for that?"*

(Billy, street preacher)

I have a friend - a man - who eats a box of Maltesers every day. I met him in Tesco recently and he had three boxes in his shopping trolley.

(Alison)

My aunt Maisie had really splashed out one Christmas and booked the family a box at the pantomime. She was quite well-oiled by the time we got to the theatre and made a big show of opening a box of Maltesers to pass around. Then, as the orchestra was warming up, she leaned over the balcony parapet to get a closer look, causing the Maltesers to tip out of their box and cascade down noisily on to the drums. At this, the audience looked up, Maisie waved at them extravagantly and they waved back, apparently under the impression that she was part of the show.

(Les)

If I was going to my granny's for the weekend, she'd come and get me in Glasgow and we'd go to get the Bluebird bus from the station at the top of Buchanan Street where she'd buy a pack of 20 Kensitas for herself and give me the change to get a Five Boys chocolate bar. I didn't like eating the piece with the crying boy on it so I always left that till last.

(Maureen)

I have a particular memory of "Five Boys" chocolate bars, not because I really liked them but because of the words that were on the wrapper: *"Desperation"*, *"Pacification"*, *"Expectation"*, *"Acclamation"*, *"Realization"*. What children were even familiar with those words, never mind knew what they meant?

(Michael)

When sweeties were rationed during the war, there was very little choice in the shops; you took what they had. You could get a Lucky Bag but they were rubbish. They cost thrupence, I think, and you got a lollipop, another sweet and a wee toy. And you were "lucky" if you got anything decent!

(Neil)

I can't believe I'm only just finding out now that there was a sweets ration as well as a sugar ration! I was very young at the time but I'm sure I can remember my mother telling me that only sugar was available in the shops, and not actual sweeties.

(Liz)

Dear Deedee,

Sorry about my late reply but I have
been so weak from lack of chocolate
that I've hardly been able to raise
finger to keyboard. However, I am
buoyed up by the fact that it's my
birthday tomorrow, and I have a
suspiciously oblong-shaped parcel
awaiting opening! It was delivered by
helicopter a couple of days ago but I
decided I should wait for the day.

As you guessed, I do have to get
deliveries of sweeties and chocolate
by any route possible: passing day
visitors, cruise ship passengers, work
parties, builders…

And then, of course, there is the famous St Kilda mouse to contend with. Much larger than any mainland beastie, it thunders around at night looking for any sugary goodies I have stashed away - and then we have real battles!!

Best wishes,

Sue
(Resident Ranger, National Trust for Scotland, St. Kilda, 2019))

Hi Deedee,

Despite the remoteness of our archipelago, my colleagues here on St. Kilda managed to fashion a chocolate cake decorated in Liquorice Allsorts for my birthday! Is that not pleasure on a plate?!! (I enclose a pic). The St Kilda mice didn't get a chance on that. Despite their enormous size and ingenuity, they were unable to open a full-size fridge door! (Plus it didn't last long!) The helicopter delivered chocolate bars and cards.

Sue (Resident Ranger, National Trust for Scotland, St. Kilda, 2019))

There's a story told in our family about one of our aunties - now dead - who, when given some sugared almonds as a gift, sucked the sugar coating off them and used the almonds for the top of a Dundee cake she was making.

(Carol)

We're reminded of a story about the elderly mum from Glasgow visiting her son in America and being asked on arrival at United States immigration: "Ma'am, do you have any meats, fruits or other foodstuffs with you?" "Aw son" she replied sympathetically. "Ah huvny even a wee sweetie ah can gie ye."

(Ken Smith in the Herald Diary)

One of the most traumatic things that happened when I was at primary school was a girl in our P2 class stealing some sweeties from another girl. Not only did she steal them - she ate them! Retribution was obviously required and she received two of the belt, in front of the whole class. What made it even more traumatic was that the girl whose sweets were stolen was my best friend and I had been hoping to get a few of her sweeties when we walked home together later that day.

(Jan)

About Deedee Cuddihy

Deedee Cuddihy is a journalist who was born and brought up in New York but has lived in Glasgow since the "Big Storm" of 1967 (which she slept through). Or was it 1968? After finishing art school in Glasgow, she realised being an artist would be too difficult - and being an art teacher would be even more difficult. So she became a journalist and has been one ever since. She is married to a Scotsman and has two grown up children - plus three granddaughters. "Scottish Sweetie Addicts and Chocoholics" is the 14th in her Funny Scottish Books series, the other titles including the best-selling "I Love Irn-Bru", "Only in Dundee" and "The Wee Guide to Scottish Women". She really likes tablet.